A souvenir guide

Canons Ashby

Northamptonshire

Andrew Barber

National Trust

'Antient as the Druids'

So reads the motto over the grandest fireplace in Canons Ashby, a motto inspired by the care and love felt for the place by generations of the same family, ensuring the conservation of its unique qualities.

The sepia-toned and nostalgia-infused atmosphere that many experience at Canons Ashby is the result of centuries of life carried on in this remote corner of rural England. The ordinariness of the lives of its inhabitants, the unremarkable nature of their household and the continuity of the estate through generations of one family all combine to show us a world of settled content. Indeed, the unremarkable ordinariness of Canons Ashby is its special quality, giving it the capacity to suggest a timeless past while reflecting the history of rural England.

Canons Ashby dates from a time when organised religion dominated every aspect of people's lives; through times when the real power in society lay with the property-owning classes; through the quiet revolutions of the Enclosure Acts and through the riotous times of the Civil War. It has suffered agricultural depression, industrial revolution and social upheaval, been subject to changes both violent and gradual down to the present day. All this has created a rich tapestry of rural life. Today, it is the task of the National Trust to reveal that tapestry's weave and weft, the details of the lives lived here.

From farm to family home

For the most part, the people who lived here were of the same family, the Drydens. Life started simply enough at Canons Ashby as a farmstead run by monks. When this monastery was dissolved like so many others by Henry VIII, its conversion into a family home was begun by the Cope family.

From 1551 and for the following four centuries it was the Drydens' family home. Their ambitious building plans and complex decorative schemes suggest what life was like for these modest Northamptonshire landowners, conservative-minded and often short of money. More revealing still are the writings of Sir Henry Dryden 'the Antiquary' and in the charming photographs taken by his daughter and the watercolours painted by his niece.

However, life at Canons Ashby was not all quiet contentment. In 1904 one correspondent, writing for *Country Life*, described Canons Ashby as having 'that mellow look which has been well described as having "the subtle fragrance of decay"'. Appearances are so frequently deceptive and the appearance of Canons Ashby, as we shall see, has been much modified over time, both modernised for comfort and fashion and conserved for the love of antiquity.

Above Sir Henry Dryden and his daughter Alice in the Pebble Court

Opposite The mellowed stone south front of Canons Ashby and the tower of St Mary's Church

Why Canons Ashby?

There are Ashbys scattered all over the country – five in Northamptonshire alone. It is an old word for a farmstead and consequently very common. Canons Ashby, therefore, was the canons' farmstead, but who were these canons?

An Augustinian priory was established here in the mid-12th century, between 1147 and 1151. Canons were groups of priests who worked and prayed for the souls of the lay community, differing from monks who prayed in seclusion for their own salvation. In the words of a French academic writing about 12th-century monasticism: 'the monk renders an account only for his own soul: the canons for the souls of others as well'.

Above Canons Ashby seen from across the recently restored stewponds

The evolution of the village

The priory at Canons Ashby was not large, probably never exceeding a dozen canons. Nevertheless, it attracted benefactors who gave farms, stewponds (where fish for the table were kept) and a mill. The stewponds have been recently excavated and restored. A link between them and the chain of lakes that now forms a decorative feature in the park has been confirmed by recent archaeological investigations. The mill sat at the foot of the park lakes.

The village of Canons Ashby was formed of two streets of houses that ran parallel to the modern Preston Capes road in the field to the north. At its western end stood a small, probably wooden, defensive manor house on a mound, which later came under the canons' ownership. At the opposite end, near a plentiful water supply, stood the priory, built to the east and south of the current church.

Revolutions in rural living

Little remains of either village or priory. In its heyday the village boasted 41 households, all employed working on the land or in associated professions. Farming was as tenants or in service to the canons; individuals would have had little land to cultivate in their own right.

This feudal society was rocked in the 1340s by the cataclysm of the Black Death (see box). Those who survived the outbreak found themselves in a very different society. Landlords, including monastic communities, faced a seriously depleted workforce. For a while those peasants who had suffered poverty prior to the plague found they could negotiate better rates for their labour, even taking over vacant tenancies. The feudal system that tied peasants to the land began to break down and labour became mobile for the first time.

However, the enclosure of common fields for the better farming of sheep reversed this change and reduced many to poverty once more as sheep came to dominate the rural economy. By 1535, at the dissolution of the priory, only nine tenants remained.

The Black Death

Insanitary conditions made epidemics of fatal diseases common in medieval Europe. However, the outbreak of plague in 1348 which continued until the winter of 1349/40 was greater in magnitude and broader in reach than any before or since. The Great Plague is estimated to have killed 30–60 per cent of Europe's total population in some areas and is thought to have reduced the world population from an estimated 450 million down to 350–375 million in the 14th century. In 1343 Canons Ashby had 41 households; in 1377 records show just 82 people paying the poll tax.

The Dissolution of the monasteries

To facilitate his divorce from his first wife, Henry VIII set up a breakaway version of Roman Catholicism, with himself as the Supreme Head of the Church in England. The effect on religious houses such as Canons Ashby was fatal.

Opposite St Mary's Church is a fragment of the Augustinian priory church that was seized by the Crown and sold into private ownership

Henry could not tolerate powerful landowning clerics owing primary loyalty to the Pope rather than to himself, so he decided to close all monastic houses and confiscate their considerable wealth. The process was made easier by the disrepute into which the monastic way of life had fallen by the 16th century, with many examples of decidedly un-monastic behaviour. In the case of Canons Ashby, the riotous behaviour of the students using the priory as a stopover travelling to and from the university at Oxford was a reason for the house to be suppressed.

The Copes' conversion

How much remained of the monastic buildings when Sir Francis Bryan acquired the priory lands from the Crown in 1537 is uncertain, but a year later he sold the property to Sir John Cope, who created a house out of the ruins.

Sir John laid out a garden including a mount and a terraced walk. The Copes were a prominent Puritan family in Banbury. It may have been the status of the church at Canons Ashby as a 'peculiar' (outside the bishop's control) that attracted Sir John. He chose to retain only the two western-most bays of the nave and the tower of the church, keeping a building of modest proportions in which to worship as he chose, without interference from the authorities. The rest of the considerable monastic site was quarried for building materials by him and his successors for centuries thereafter.

Although caricatured as black-suited humourless prigs in their religious observance (see box), Puritan gentry like the Copes and subsequent owners the Drydens were as keen as any of their class to keep up with the latest fashions. Certainly social ambition was not lacking in the Puritan generations of the Drydens, as we shall see.

Puritanism

In the early 16th century the powerful Roman Catholic Church faced rebellion. Reformers (or Protestants) accused it of straying from Christ's teaching as revealed in the Bible. The Protestant Reformation splintered into a variety of groups, which took the word of Biblical teaching more or less literally. Puritans were the most literal believers in Biblical truth. As is always the case, these religious differences also split people along political lines. With the exception of Mary I's brief reign, Puritanism flourished under Henry's heirs. Puritans demanded the removal of all that stood between the soul and salvation. This included structures of church and state, which sought to impose hierarchy and orthodoxy, and the host of saints, statues and rituals that accompanied Roman Catholic (and Henry's Anglican) worship. Conflict was inevitable and was fought out in the Civil Wars of 1642–52.

St Mary's Church

The tower of St Mary's Church is visible for miles around. The monastic buildings started on a grand scale in about 1250, but the effects of religious conflict and subsequent demolitions have left just part of the nave and the tower, forming the present church.

The remaining rump of the church at Canons Ashby has been dismissed as having no architectural interest. This is not entirely true: the delicacy and complexity of the carved arcading that enriches the west front of the church is the work of a skilled hand, using whitewash and the natural tints of the stone to produce a delicate and pleasing effect.

The window above the door appears heavy and perhaps rather oversized. It was a late alteration undertaken by the canons before they were ejected. The east wall marks the point at which Sir John Cope's demolition of the church stopped (it had extended a further 100 feet). The wall is his, whilst the south wall appears to have been rebuilt by Edward Dryden in the early 18th century, to judge by the classical pilasters that divide its length. (A pilaster is a vertical strip of masonry, often with base and capital, attached to a wall to give the appearance of a column.)

Pageantry and heraldry

The plain, whitewashed interior suited the Puritan tastes of the Copes and early Drydens, but belies what may have been a far more colourful interior before the Reformation. The fragmentary painting of cherubs holding back a

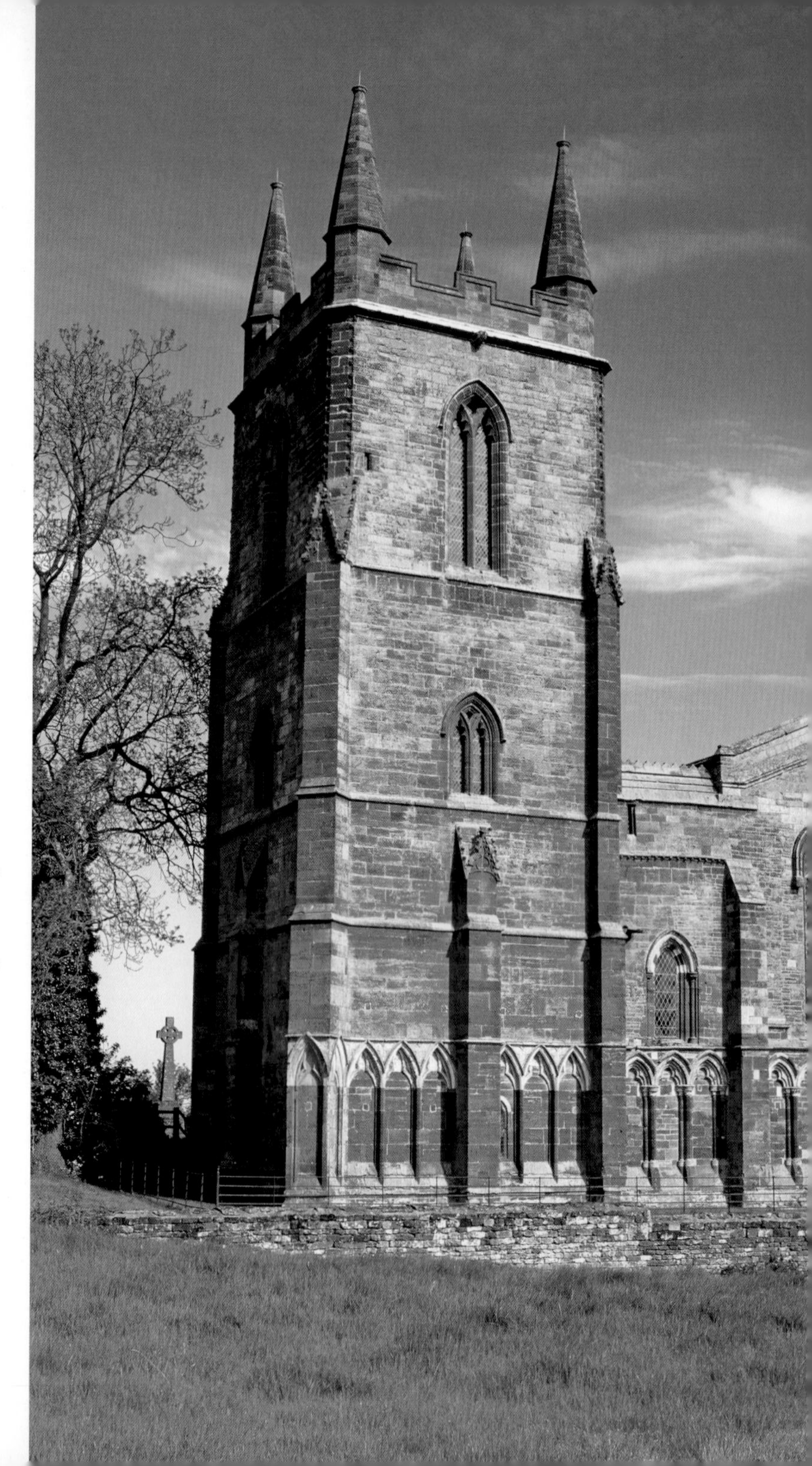

Left The west front of St Mary's Church with its arcading dating to its 13th-century origins as a monastery

curtain on the east wall was painted later, probably for Edward Dryden by his cousin, Elizabeth Creed, a skilled amateur artist (see page 29).

The painted heraldic boards, called hatchments, record and advertise the deaths of members of the Dryden family. They were hung on the outside of the house shortly after the death before coming to rest high up in the church. Sir Robert Dryden's sword, helmet, gauntlets and pennant hang on the south wall. The habit of sending military and heraldic symbols to the grave with deceased warriors was already archaic by 1708, but Sir Robert's funeral was of a magnificence equivalent to that of a medieval knight (which, of course, he was not).

The tower is an empty shell, its interior a victim of a skirmish in the Civil War (see the box on page 21). Beside the organ is a memorial stone for Gervase Jackson-Stops who, beyond any other single person, was responsible for the rescue of Canons Ashby in the 1980s (see page 51).

Above right High up on the walls of the interior hang heraldic boards celebrating the Dryden family

Right The memorial to Sir Robert Dryden set in the floor of the aisle

Tudor Origins

Pictured A view of the Pebble Court including the tower and the range containing the Great Hall

'Pull down to the ground all the walls of the churches, steeples, cloisters, fraters, dorters, chapter-houses, with all other houses, saving them that be necessary for a farmer...'

Such were the instructions given to Henry VIII's Commissioners for the Dissolution of the Abbeys. It appears that the commissioners followed them to the letter at Canons Ashby. Initially it was to a farmhouse that John Dryden brought his bride, Elizabeth Cope, after their marriage in 1551. It was from such humble beginnings that they set about improving, enlarging and creating a house that became Canons Ashby.

It is difficult to see evidence for the farmhouse now; a stray reference in a document of 1573 is all that we have to link it to the current house. In this John agreed a lease with Edward Cope, Sir John Cope's heir, that included permission to lay new water pipes from the monastic spring, the Norwell (North Well), to his own 'Mansion House, lately Wylkyn's farm...'.

Wylkyn's farmhouse has been identified with the north-west corner of the current house (see page 12). What John built on his newly acquired land was a tower and adjacent west wing, possibly attached by a single-storey corridor (where the Great Hall is) to the farmhouse.

Standing out from the crowd

The tower is a strange feature to find in Northamptonshire. Semi-defensive with its great thick walls and small windows, such structures were more normally found in the lawless northern borderlands in the 15th and 16th centuries. Its arrival in Northamptonshire is not fully understood, nor is that of John himself, about whom we know very little, except that he came from Cumberland. It is possible that the healthy trade in wool and sheep farming brought him here (see box).

The tower's roughness is only partially tamed by the west wing in which John and Elizabeth probably had their Parlour and Best Chamber, confining everyday living to the smaller, more easily heated rooms of the tower. Today, the upper rooms in the tower are not open to visitors but form a holiday flat bookable through the Landmark Trust.

Sheep stealing

The only other reference in the records to John Dryden is about sheep, which gives a possible motive for his coming to Northamptonshire. It is an accusation that he led a gang of rustlers who stole the sheep of John Bocher of Adstone. John vigorously defended himself, denying the charge and claiming that Bocher was delusional. No more is heard of the case, so some sort of accommodation must have been reached.

The Pebble Court

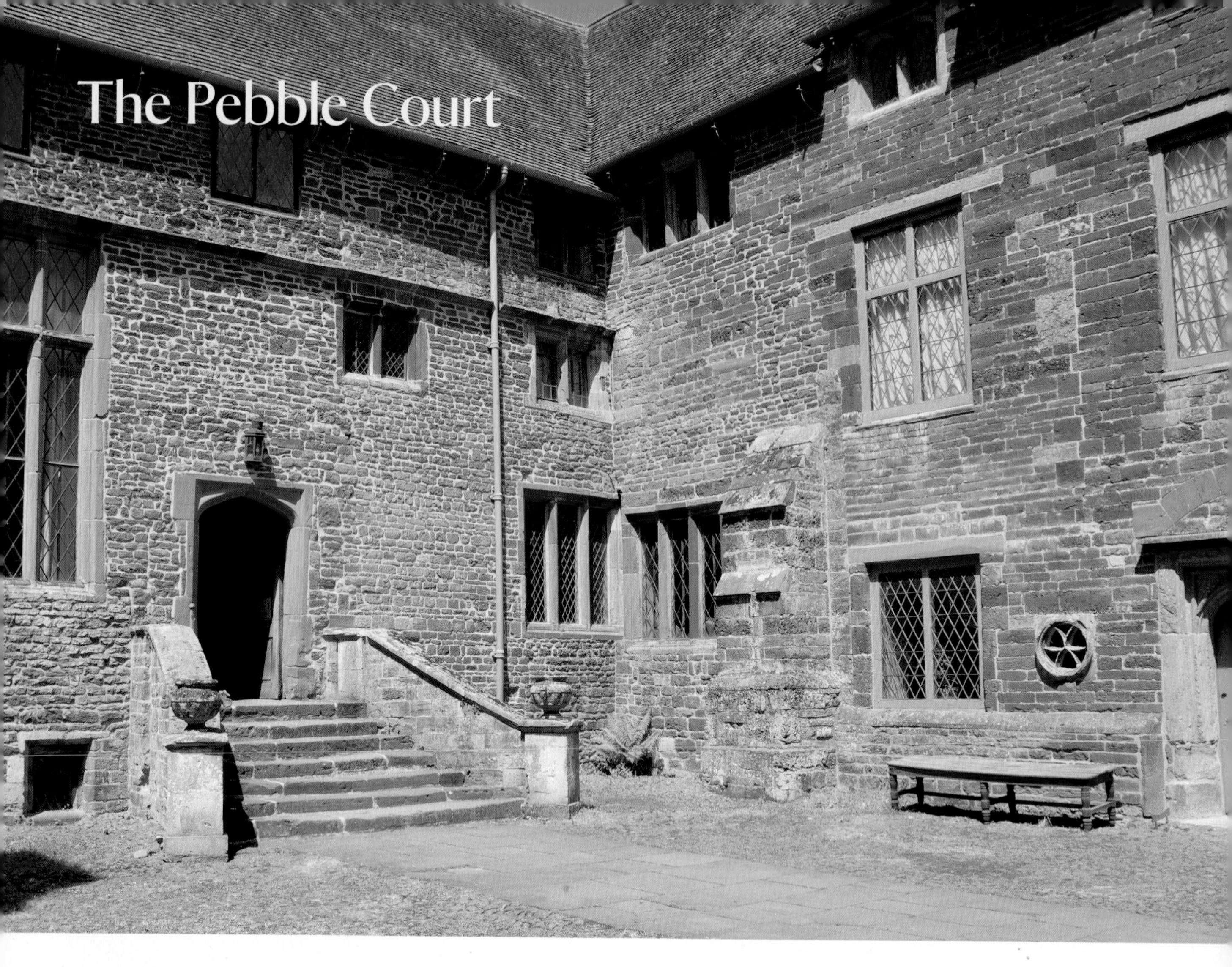

The architecture of Canons Ashby reveals itself like a detective story with disparate clues suggesting evidence of its building history in tiny details. A good place to appreciate the complexity of the house's building is the Pebble Court.

The great tower that constituted part of John Dryden's first phase sits in the south-west corner. Note the sloping stonework of the Great Hall range giving light to one of the tower windows (now blocked) – an indication that the window probably existed first and the wall was contorted to accommodate it. The vertical straight line in the masonry adjacent to the tower on the south side indicates that the range to the east was added to the pre-existing tower.

Recent investigations have shown that several generations of the Drydens believed in recycling. There was, after all, a hoard of materials offered

Opposite The Pebble Court's north-west corner reveals a patchwork of building material

Below A photograph of an unknown servant in the Pebble Court showing a re-used window and door moulding from the priory

by the disused monastic buildings to which, after a lease of 1573, John Dryden had access. Stone and particularly carved mouldings were valuable; very few of the apparently early windows in the house have correctly matched mouldings, indicating that they were scavenged in bits and matched on site.

Here are some of the best and most obvious examples of the recycling habits of the Drydens: both the door case in the centre of the north wing and the little porthole window beside it are complete pieces of late medieval work, made originally for somewhere else and later inserted into the fabric of the house. The bigger windows on the first floor of the north range are later insertions, probably indicative of large-scale remodelling undertaken by Edward Dryden in the early 18th century (see 'Edward's Improvements').

Humble origins

As already stated, the external evidence for Wylkyn's Farm, the first building on the site initially occupied by John and Elizabeth, is not at all obvious. In the north-west corner, where the farmhouse stood, the disarrangement of the masonry following the insertion of many windows suggests large-scale alteration. The use of a buttress to shore up the old walls in this corner during alterations was probably the work of John's son and successor, Erasmus Dryden.

On the east side, where the entrance tunnel brings visitors into the Pebble Court, the low, uneven profile of the roof suggests the character of a late-medieval thatched farm building, whilst the exposed beam-end visible towards the right-hand end halfway up the east wall is evidence of former mud walling (which would have been thicker than the later stone wall and would have covered the beam end). High up on the east end of the south range preparatory work for a higher new wing with a more regular roofline to replace the old range remain, a reminder that funds were usually in short supply for the Drydens and that not all building projects came to fruition.

Erasmus extended the two 'legs' of his father's house eastwards to meet the former barn, creating the courtyard house as we see it today.

The H-shaped house

The H-shaped house that John and his son Erasmus created can be seen in the Pebble Court, in the straight vertical joints in the masonry to the left of the tower and opposite (though less clearly) by the buttress.

John and Elizabeth's new wing was linked to the farmhouse by the creation of the Great Hall sometime before John's death in 1584. Decoratively this is now almost entirely Edward Dryden's room, who made extensive alterations to Canons Ashby in the 18th century. The only remaining internal features of John Dryden's Great Hall are the stone Tudor fireplace, the blocked doorway to the Green Court and the blocked twin accesses to the former farmhouse placed centrally on the north wall – all of which share exactly the same moulding profiles (so not recycled!). A timber screen across the north end of the room, forming a passage linking the two doors to the exterior, would have been a dominant feature of this room, possibly including a gallery above, but it was swept away, along with the raised dais at the opposite end, when Edward completely remodelled the space in 1708–12.

Below The only remaining Tudor detail of the Great Hall created by John Dryden is the stone fireplace

Archaeological evidence has proved that the Great Hall was never open to the roof timbers in the manner of some Elizabethan halls. Above it is the Long Gallery which has a run of rooms along its west side in which fragments of early painted work survive, further indicating that the Long Gallery is an original feature of John Dryden's building.

The kitchen extension

The Kitchen was created by John Dryden but its extension to the east, creating an H-plan, was probably undertaken by John's son and heir, Erasmus. At the same time Erasmus improved the natural light in the Great Hall by enlarging the windows. In the Kitchen are two pieces of furniture, which, whilst they don't date to John's period, are precise replicas of a table and a buffet that did. These were recorded here in drawings and in photographs taken by Sir Henry in the 19th century.

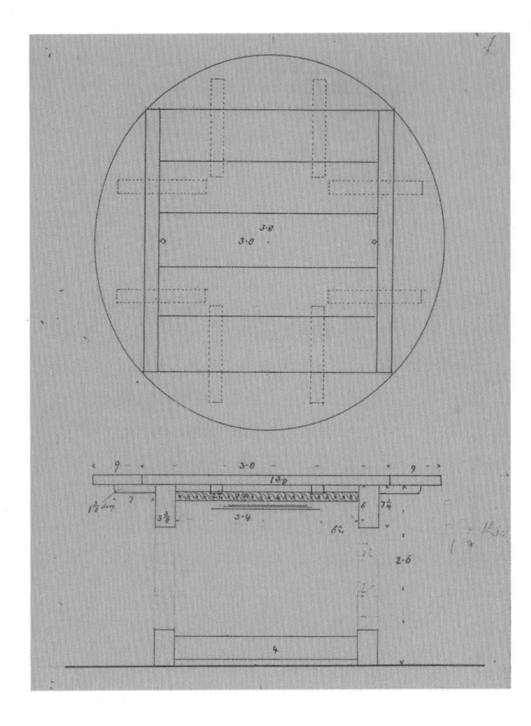

Right A drawing of the kitchen table by Sir Henry Dryden that allowed a precise replica to be built

Below Leading off the Great Hall is the Kitchen

The heart of the house

With so many centuries of occupation, the interiors at Canons Ashby have inevitably changed in form and function. The space now occupied by the Servants' Hall was the Winter Parlour when in family use and formed the heart of Wylkyn's Farm.

When the first Dryden, John, came to it, the Winter Parlour was divided horizontally with a mezzanine floor. When the current room was formed is uncertain; the bay window on the north side is later than John's time and is probably the work of his son Erasmus in the early 17th century, as it matches the full-height bay at the other end of the wing (both appear to be later additions to the front). The most striking element in the room is the painted panelling, a rare and most unusual survival which, from its subject matter, must be of John and Elizabeth's time.

Elizabeth's line

The subject matter is classical and heraldic. The quotation of authors from antiquity such as Seneca (as in the top frieze, offering injunctions to healthy and moral living) was the mark of a Renaissance education, and something suited to the puritanical leanings of both the Cope and Dryden families. Emblems containing allusions to the great thinkers of the classical world would have amused, instructed and impressed the Drydens and their guests. Such motifs were commonly included in the decoration of Elizabethan great chambers; a far later (and far grander) example is to be found in the plaster frieze of the High Great Chamber at Hardwick Hall in Derbyshire, which is full of allegory and wordplay for the amusement and edification of the educated Elizabethan mind.

The largest part of the scheme is devoted to a heraldic arrangement that traces some of the most important familial connections of Elizabeth Cope. The scheme is incomplete but contains reference to families who had connections with the Copes (the Spensers, Bacons and Cecils) going back several generations from around 1570. The selection seems to have favoured Elizabeth's more illustrious ancestors but, as yet, the precise criterion is unclear. What is not in doubt is that the panelling was fitted to the room after its creation and must have been in another space first. As it celebrates Elizabeth's lineage, it is reasonable to think that it was originally fitted in one of the two larger chambers first built by John and Elizabeth – rooms that became the Dining and Tapestry Rooms in Edward's remodelling of the early 18th century – only moving to its current position when Erasmus created his far grander Great Chamber (see pages 18–19).

Above The room formerly known as the Winter Parlour, created in the 1580s, was downgraded to a dining room for the upper servants in about 1710

Early decoration

Above the Servants' Hall, in a room now shown as the Dryden Sitting Room, survive two fragments of decorative painting, both dating from this early period of development.

The first is a ceiling painting of family crests, similar to those in the Servants' Hall, featuring coats of arms. Again this is incomplete and its heraldic meaning uncertain. The decorative grid in which the arms sit was taken from a book by the Italian architect Serlio, in which he set out glazing patterns or designs for knot gardens. It is unlikely that the decorators, or indeed John and Elizabeth, will have possessed such an exotic volume, but they must have had access to a copy, perhaps through Elizabeth's grand relations.

The other is a wall painting, badly damaged but still discernible in its overall design and in some details. It is painted in monochrome and shows a family kneeling at prayer, men to the left and women to the right. The scene is set in an interior with mullioned windows not unlike those in the smart new rooms John and Elizabeth had built in their new wing. At the centre, beneath a sunburst containing the Hebrew letters symbolising God, is the coat of arms of Dryden impaling that of Cope, signifying John's marriage to Elizabeth. The whole is presented as a theatrical stage with a cherub holding up a curtain above the cornice as if presenting the scene to the onlooker.

Tapestry-like, the left-hand side has a border overflowing with fruit. Over it, painted on the beam, are improving couplets in Latin, as in the Servants' Hall. Details such as the clock (symbolising the value of a well-regulated life) and the caged bird (symbolising the human soul imprisoned by ignorance until released by an understanding of the truth of God's Word) were common motifs in 16th-century iconography, symbolic reminders of the fleeting passage of life and the need to live it well.

Above Part of the ceiling painting dating to John and Elizabeth's development and decoration of the house

Below Traces of a Tudor wall painting showing a family kneeling at prayer in an Elizabethan interior

Puritanical pride

Erasmus, John and Elizabeth's eldest surviving son, succeeded to the property on his father's death in 1584. Canons Ashby offered Erasmus the freedom to worship as he chose and he took a care to enhance and embellish his home.

Erasmus kept the Puritan divine, John Dod, as part of his household from 1608–31 and had him preach in the church in defiance of the official intolerance of non-conformity, safe in the protection afforded him by the 'peculiar' status of his church at Canons Ashby.

He continued his father's ambitious programme of building over the decades around the turn of the century, bringing the old service range of Wylkyn's Farm into the house. It is likely that at this time the mud walls of the original farm building were rebuilt in stone.

The north wing had a grand chamber constructed on its top floor lit by the projecting oriel window still visible on the east front. In its 16th-century form it was a double-height chamber with an ambitious double-barrel vault, fragmentary evidence for which survives after later alterations and floor-level changes.

Above Erasmus's great decorative triumph was painted over until this scheme in imitation of marble was revealed by the National Trust in the 1980s

Erasmus's ambitions
Erasmus was a martyr to his politics and religion, being twice imprisoned for failing to support King Charles I's attempts to fund his rule with illegal taxes. Nevertheless, at the age of 66 he bought a baronetcy for the large sum of £1,100. When a servant's annual wage was a matter of a few pounds and the cost of a good horse was not much more, such a sum is truly astonishing, and puts paid to any suggestion that Puritans were socially or financially retiring.

Grand statements

In the south range, Erasmus's Great Chamber (the current Drawing Room) also boasted a great projecting bay, nearly all traces of which were lost in the early 18th-century remodelling of the south front by Edward (see pages 25–27). However, elements of decorative plasterwork from the flat ceiling of the bay, echoing that in the frieze of the fireplace, were uncovered in the 1980s. Erasmus's ceiling for this room – another barrel vault, but single this time – has also been superseded, but his great decorative triumph, the fireplace, survives.

A grand architectural monument embellished with carving and colour, the columns are enriched to make them appear as black marble, whilst the ground is speckled to evoke a red marble effect. This painted decorative scheme was revealed by the National Trust in the 1980s having been covered over for at least 200 years.

Erasmus's decoration

Another discovery by the National Trust was a scheme of scenes painted *en grisaille* (in grey with subtle shadowing and black and white highlights) above a high, coloured dado in the adjacent chamber called Spenser's Room.

This painted scheme, consisting of two fragmentary scenes and traces of others depicting passages from the Biblical Book of Kings, tells the story of King Jeroboam and his encounter with 'the Man of God who came out of Judah', which had dire consequences for both. This and the other patterned and coloured work in the room was covered over by the installation of panelling in the 18th century; however, Erasmus's coat of arms, high up on the east wall over where a window once stood, confirms that this decoration is his. The original doorway from the adjoining room is now blocked, and on its plaster face charming doodles of an 18th-century clergyman and an attractive young woman imply far more than is actually said.

(For more on Spenser's Room and Edward Dryden's remodelling of it, see pages 34–35.)

An elevated stairway

Erasmus installed a new staircase to his Great Chamber. The grandeur of the panelled posts topped with spiked grenades and the bobbin-reel turned balusters is only partially eclipsed by the muddle of floor levels that resulted from accommodating the original spiral staircase above and below as well as later floor-level adjustments.

Above The grand staircase installed by Erasmus to lead up to his Great Chamber

Below 18th-century graffiti of a clergyman and a fashionable young woman in Spenser's Room

Vaulting ambition

Erasmus died in 1632, leaving Canons Ashby to the eldest of his six children. Sir John, 2nd Baronet, married for a third time shortly after. In celebration of the marriage, he put a new vaulted ceiling into his father's Great Chamber, what is now the Drawing Room.

This most decorative of plaster ceilings contains four major panels in its strapwork pattern, one in the centre of each side of the four-part vault. In one of these, in pride of place over the fireplace, he put his coat of arms emblazoned in colours impaling those of his new bride, Honor Bevill.

The structure of the ceiling is ambitious, centring on a drop pendant from which a chandelier would have hung. It resembles the plaster ceilings of mid- to late Elizabethan houses such as Heslington Hall in York and Bramall Hall near Stockport. Another example at Blickling Hall in Norfolk is nearer in date, but the Canons Ashby ceiling is a late example of its kind, with backward-looking (though very fine) decoration. In such a remote corner of rural England, perhaps this should not come as a surprise.

However, that is not the only, nor indeed the most interesting, element in this unique ceiling. The decoration of the other three panels consists of an elaborate strapwork cartouche centring on a bust-length female figure in masquing dress. Masques were exotic entertainments, featuring lavish costumes, scenery, music and dancing, that were popular in

the court of Elizabeth and her successors. The masquing costumes depicted in the ceiling at Canons Ashby sport elaborate headdresses, martial breastplates and naked breasts, all features that were popular in the costume of female actors in masques (Queen Anne, wife of James I, came in for heavy censure for her participation in masques). Masques were not royal and aristocratic entertainments alone, but were imitated on a smaller scale in gentry houses such as Canons Ashby, so it is highly appropriate that such an apparently licentious decorative detail should be so prominently displayed in Sir John's newly refurbished Great Chamber.

Quiet consolidation

Sir Robert Dryden, the 3rd Baronet, succeeded his father and seems to have lived a quiet life at Canons Ashby, shunning the public stage and forbearing to alter anything in the house. This might be thought surprising considering the degree of damage done to country houses during the Civil War; Canons Ashby must have been lucky.

He did, however, achieve the purchase of the Cope mansion on the site of the priory, bringing the entire monastic site into the ownership of the Drydens. It is probable at this time that the pair of carved heraldic panels that celebrates the marriage of Sir John Cope (John Dryden's father-in-law) to his third wife, Margaret, now over the fireplace in the Book Room, came to Canons Ashby. The Cope house was dismantled and one wonders how much of it was recycled as part of the next phase of improvements that overtook Canons Ashby like a whirlwind the moment Sir Robert was laid to rest in his ornately and expensively decorated tomb.

Opposite Erasmus's elaborate plasterwork ceiling commissioned for his Great Chamber, now the Drawing Room

Puritan and Parliamentarian

Sir John was as devout a Puritan as his father and grandfather. He was reported to be 'very furious against the clergy' and took Parliament's side during the Civil War. An episode from that time tells how a Parliamentarian troop, quartered in the house in 1644, was forced to retreat into the church by Royalists from Banbury. Here the Parliamentarians held out for some time before being smoked out and taken prisoner. The tower of the church remains an empty shell as a result of the firing of the building. Lady Dryden provided mutton pies for the Roundheads, leaving them on the garden wall, but they were carried off by the victorious Cavaliers instead. Sir John represented the county in Parliament throughout the years of the Civil War and for most of the period of the Commonwealth, surviving the purges and religious mania of the times, dying peacefully in 1658.

Below The Dryden coat of arms set into the plasterwork ceiling of the Drawing Room

Edward's Improvements

Edward enjoyed his inheritance for just under a decade, yet he wrought more changes on the face of Canons Ashby than had been done since his great-grandfather a century earlier.

Edward was not the obvious heir; Sir Robert had cousins who had prior claim and all of whom succeeded in turn to the baronetcy, whilst Edward enjoyed ownership of Canons Ashby. The last of these absent baronets, Edward's father, Sir Erasmus, 6th Baronet, outlived him by a year, so Edward never succeeded to the title.

Why Sir Robert chose to leave the house and estates to his distant nephew is unknown, but the reason possibly lay with the competing candidates above him: two were men already in their sixties and the third, the poet John Dryden's son, was unmarried and, worse still, a Roman Catholic (although the two evidently overcame their religious differences when he came to live with his cousin at Canons Ashby). Edward, on the other hand, had a wealthy wife, children, was a Protestant and carried on a successful trade as a grocer in Westminster.

Right Edward Dryden redesigned the west front and the Green Court which it overlooks

Below Over the fireplace in the Great Hall Edward installed this board trumpeting a militaristic history

All change

Inside the house there is scarcely a space Edward left untouched. The Great Hall bears his decorative stamp, with the smart chequer-board stone floor and the grand new entrance from the Green Court. In the Kitchen the great pier on the left as you enter from the Great Hall and the grand triple-arched cooking hearth date to his period. In the Servants' Hall his remodelling of the windows in the west front would have occasioned further rearrangement of the heraldic panelling. He created a grand panelled chamber on the first floor of the north wing (now part of the Dryden family's flat and not shown to visitors) with a bake house below, the flue for which destroyed his great-grandfather's even grander double-barrel vaulted chamber above.

Past glories

Some of Edward's most consciously old-fashioned furnishings are in the Great Hall. It was possibly his second cousin, Elizabeth Creed, who supplied him with the board over his grand fireplace painted with trophies, drums, pikes and other accoutrements of war. Maybe she (or her daughter Elizabeth Steward) painted the dummy board guardsman, a companion on long lonely evenings in the country, who wears the uniform of a Scot's Guardsman, a regiment first raised for George I in 1715. As the guardsman features in the inventory taken at Edward's death in 1717, it dates him very precisely. The inventory also records armaments hung on the walls: an oddly militaristic form of decoration for a grocer, or perhaps the sign of a young man determined to establish his credentials as the heir to an ancient family?

A Classical renaissance

Below The west front of Canons Ashby with wooden cupola and clock added by Edward Dryden in the early 18th century

Edward probably did not expect to inherit from his uncle Robert, but when he did, he set about his inheritance with zeal and ambition, making improvements to both house and gardens and bringing them near to completion within nine years.

Edward created a grand entrance on the west front. This had been John Dryden's most imposing creation: a squared 'U' front, with projecting gabled wings at each end of his new Great Hall. However, his front door, proudly bearing the carved insignia of his and his wife's families, sat to one end of the hall, thus off-centre to the main façade. Edward created a new door centrally with a grand door case surmounted by a large and beautifully worked coat of arms cast in lead (and probably originally painted). He installed new, symmetrically placed lead downpipes and gave them striking spiky coronets at each intersection.

Edward also changed the windows; in his new Dining Room and what was now the Servants' Hall, each situated in the projecting wings, he replaced the old mullioned windows with pairs of that invention, recently imported from France – sash windows. Finally, to give his grand new front greater impact and architectural coherence, he covered up all the evidence of his changes under a uniting layer of render. It was later generations who blocked the sashes in the Servants' Hall and revealed John and Elizabeth's original entrance doorway.

Sash windows

Now such a normal part of many old buildings, it is hard to understand how revolutionary sash windows must have been when they first appeared in this country. Early examples survive at Belton House (Lincolnshire) and Nunnington Hall (Yorkshire) where Viscount Preston had been ambassador to Versailles for the short-lived reign of James II, bringing back the fashion for this regularly shaped, glazed and (compared to the old casement windows) remarkably draught-proof form of fenestration. Conveniently, the sash window also fitted very well with the symmetrical façades that the prevailing taste for classical Baroque architecture demanded.

A remodelled face

To the south Edward made his most dramatic alterations, creating an almost entirely new front (pictured overleaf). To John's wing containing the Dining and Tapestry rooms and his son Erasmus's Great Chamber wing (conveniently differentiated by the surviving mouldings on the mullions of the basement windows to either side of the tower steps) Edward gave a completely new face. He did this by removing a projecting bay and replacing existing mullion windows with a plethora of sashes, facing the walls in smooth (expensive and definitely not recycled) ashlar masonry.

He tried to give the whole front, which faced his brand new formal terraced garden, an air of fashionable symmetry but the old house fought back, refusing to allow symmetry to prevail despite Edward's introduction of rhythmic lead downpipes (again with spiky coronets) and a grand new doorway with steps up from the garden. The spacing of the sashes stubbornly refused to work and the conundrum of the asymmetrically placed old tower could not be answered without wholesale rebuilding.

In the end Edward had to settle for a hybrid front, half modern Baroque swagger, half old Tudor solidity, a far from heavenly architectural marriage, but entirely in tune with the character of the place: individual, charming and without pretension.

Below The lead downpipes added by Edward and drawn by Sir Henry over 100 years later

Fashion and finance

It is interesting to speculate why Edward didn't go further and remodel the whole of the south front in smooth cut stone – including the tower – and indeed why he chose the cheaper option of render for his smart new entrance front.

Expense is the obvious explanation. Much of Edward's work can be seen as gaining the maximum effect for the minimum interference. However, Edward was a successful businessman, unlike his predecessors, and brought the confidence of 'new' money to his inheritance.

Intriguingly another possibility presents itself. Edward rejoiced in the antiquity of his Dryden heritage, inventing a new motto 'Antient as the Druids' for himself (note the deliberately archaic spelling of 'ancient'). It is quite possible that a respect for the work of his ancestors moderated his modernising. He saved (and played up) some aspects of the antiquity in his ancestral home, whilst introducing the metropolitan taste for classical order. Was this deliberate? We cannot be sure in his case, but certainly later generations of Drydens sensed the antiquity of the place and strove to preserve and enhance it.

Seeking symmetry

The improvements carried out by Edward Dryden between 1708 and 1712 were done in the prevailing Baroque fashion. In England the Baroque taste sought order through the use of motifs from classical Rome and Greece, such as columns, pediments and scrolls to give balance, order and proportion to architecture. Above all, symmetry was desired, within which complex rhythms and repeating motifs could be arranged into a satisfying whole. This didn't really work out here for Edward, although perhaps his west front, looking onto the Green Court (see previous page), came nearest to achieving the goal.

On the face of it

The outside of Canons Ashby wears a variety of styles, introduced by various Drydens. The north front, facing the Preston Capes road is a mixture of periods; to either end the pair of full height bays seem to date after John Dryden's initial alterations to Wylkyn's Farm and probably belong to his son Erasmus's creation of the complete wing in the early 17th century. The large windows in the Kitchen are probably Edward's as (most definitely) are the sashes. The two-storey bay at the left-hand (eastern) end was blocked by Edward, to be reopened at the end of the 19th century as part of Sir Henry the Antiquary's sensitive curatorship of his ancient property.

Piles of cut stone from the quarry at Helmdon lie in the paddock by the Coach House and bear witness to the Reverend Sir Henry's ambitions to rebuild the east front of his house in a regular Tudor form, abolishing the rude irregularity and low undulating profile of the ancient range. Perhaps fortunately for current tastes and for the romance of Canons Ashby, the Reverend's plans came to nothing, a victim of his struggles to maintain order in his finances.

In the gable of the left-hand (southern) wing are scars in the masonry and a large exposed timber lintel, bearing witness to alterations including former window openings in Spenser's Room on the first floor – possibly even a projecting oriel with a pair of Edward's sashes beneath it matching his arrangement on the north gable.

Opposite Edward attempted to impose symmetry on the south front but features such as the original Tudor tower refused to comply

Quality craftsmanship

On the ground floor of the south front, where he had wrought such changes externally, Edward made further radical improvements.

The Dining Room, entirely of Edward's creation, is robustly masculine and beautifully executed (note the fine carving of the capitals on the west wall). John Bridges, the 18th-century historian, wrote of this room in *The History and Antiquities of Northamptonshire*: 'It is entirely floored and wainscoted [panelled] with the timber of a single oak which grew in that lordship.'

The 'landscape' glass over the mantel is fixed at such an angle to allow those facing the fireplace at dinner to enjoy views down the garden behind them. The rest of the contents of the room largely post-date Edward's time, although the portraits mostly record his wife's familial connections with service to the royal household.

Below The decidedly masculine Dining Room was Edward's creation

John Dryden, Poet Laureate
'Glorious John' Dryden, celebrated poet and author of epic satires such as *Absalom and Achitophel*, was Edward's uncle and father of Sir Erasmus Henry, 5th Baronet, who came to live with Edward at Canons Ashby. His portrait hangs in the Dining Room, although his direct connections with the place are few. He may have harboured romantic feelings for his cousin Honor, but if he did there is no evidence that any courtship took place here. His visits to Northamptonshire took him to his own family home at Tichmarsh. Perhaps his Catholic leanings kept him from Canons Ashby. Whatever the truth of the matter, the poet married an earl's daughter (unhappily) and Honor remained unmarried.

A skilful deception

At the far end of the south front is the Painted Parlour (now shown as Sir Henry's Museum). Here fancy took flight and Elizabeth Creed created for her cousin a little jewel box of a room. Grandly conceived, and yet on a minute scale, its partly real and partly painted perspective can deceive the eye even on close inspection. The cornice, for instance, is a simple piece of board set at an angle to unite ceiling and wall planes, yet Elizabeth Creed (or her daughter, Elizabeth Steward) with a deft brush and an intimate knowledge of paint created the illusion of three-dimensional marble mouldings with consummate brilliance.

The gilt overmantel mirror is original to the room, but little else is. The three caned high-back walnut chairs are some of the finest of their kind, illustrating the skills of the metropolitan craftsmen from whom Edward had begun to order furnishings for his newly decorated interiors (see also the Tapestry Room, overleaf). The white floorboards are sycamore, newly installed in 1983 as the original floor (also sycamore) had been destroyed by woodworm.

Above Elizabeth Creed, who was responsible for the decoration of her cousin's Painted Parlour

Below Edward's concern for quality and craftsmanship can be seen in his choice of furnishings such as this high-back walnut chair and in the skilfully deceptive decorative scheme

A fondness for fabrics

Upstairs, Edward's main contribution to this part of the house was the creation of the Tapestry Room. Like the armaments he chose to display in his Great Hall, his choice of tapestries here demonstrate a fondness for a self-consciously old-fashioned look.

Here Edward blocked up the original mullioned windows to the north and west and covered them with tapestry. His uniform south front of sash windows exposed an unevenness in floor levels, so window seats were introduced in front of the sashes to disguise the awkward effect. The panelling is from Sir Erasmus's time. Less coherent and thoroughgoing than other rooms that Edward tackled, fragments of earlier decoration survive (see the little bit of painted cornice visible near the fireplace), a reminder perhaps that Edward's was an untimely death and that the Tapestry Room was still 'work in progress' when he died.

Fine furnishings

The set of needlework chairs, settee and fire screen are a remarkable survival in extremely good condition (for the story of their discovery and recovery, see the box on page 53). In an archive sadly lacking in details of Edward's acquisitions, it is wonderful to find a record of Thomas Phill, 'Upholsterer to Her late Majesty, Queen Anne and also to George I and George II' submitting an invoice that includes £7 7s 0d for '6 wallnuttree back chaires, frames of ye newest fashion, Stufft up in Lynnen' and 'ffore making ye needlework covers and fixeing ym on ye chaires' ('making' here probably meaning 'fitting'). The embroiderers copied patterns of delft vases (highly fashionable at the time) filled with exotic flowers.

Also of this period and of restrained beauty is the pair of giltwood mirrors, carved in low relief in gesso (plaster) and water-gilded to give a brilliance that would have sparkled in the candlelight of the attached sconces.

Opposite In this room tapestries were used by Edward Dryden as we might use wallpaper

Below An embroidered needlework walnut chair incorporating bouquets of flowers and Delft vases upholstered by Thomas Phill in 1714

Consciously old-fashioned

At the dawn of the Georgian age, tapestry was fast going out of fashion as a furnishing fabric. By this time, when tapestry rooms were created, as here and at Doddington Hall, Lincolnshire, a few decades later, they were conscious statements of antiquity and 'ancientness'. We don't know if Edward inherited the tapestries for this room or bought them (if he did, they would have been second-hand). Either way, his ruthless treatment of them, almost as woven wallpaper, cutting them to fit the room and ignoring any sense of scheme or subject matter, was typical of those aiming for a decorative effect rather than displaying the objects for their intrinsic value. Worse was to follow: as the condition of at least one of the tapestries deteriorated, it fell off the wall and ended up, somewhat ignominiously, as bedding for one of the Drydens' tenants' dogs. It was rescued by the National Trust and conserved. Pictured is the room in the 1960s before its restoration.

Edward's Great Chamber

Edward's major alteration, as discussed previously, was to remove Sir Erasmus's large bay that thrust out from his Great Chamber (now known as the Drawing Room) over the south garden.

There is some question as to whether this bay was a full-height one (like those on the north front) or an oriel (like that on the east front). A complete run of Elizabethan basement windows below, apparently undisturbed, suggests the latter, although archaeological evidence is inconclusive.

Whichever is the case, the effect on Erasmus's Great Chamber must have been enormous. Fragments of decorative plasterwork recovered during the 1980s show that the bay was united decoratively with the main part of the room, whilst performing its duty as a smaller 'room' within the greater one to which select company could retire to converse. Edward's other intervention was to install his painted coats of arms, with their newly minted motto – 'Antient as the Druids' – over the mantel.

Right This family portrait by Jonathan Richardson the Elder is thought to depict Edward and Elizabeth with their children John, Bevill and Mary

Statements of wealth

The silver tea kettle is part of the trappings of his elevation to gentry status with which Edward provided himself and his wife. The engraved arms are theirs, the maker is Thomas Sadler and the date is 1712.

The large family portrait was acquired in the belief that it depicts Edward and his family, which it might well, but the children are too few and seem to be the wrong ages in relation to each other. More research is required.

Probably the finest piece of furniture in the house is to be found here: a 'seaweed' marquetry cabinet-on-chest, which shows the highest qualities of craftsmanship (see box below). The cabinet was taken to Rhodesia (now Zimbabwe) when some of the Dryden family emigrated. There it survived possible attack by termites and extreme desiccation, both dangerous conditions for veneered furniture.

Left Silver tea kettle with burner dated 1712 and bearing the coat of arms of Edward and Elizabeth Dryden

The art of marquetry

The taste for exotic and coloured woods decorating furniture became fashionable in Elizabethan England. It was only in the second half of the 17th century that the skills of craftsmen enabled them to create pictures and patterns in exotic woods that did not rely on the laborious and limiting process of inlaying into the wood. Better results could be achieved creating a multi-wood veneer, like a jigsaw, that covered the surface completely. Marquetry came in all shapes and sizes, on chests, clocks, chairs, frames, tables and cabinets and in a multitude of forms, floral, pictorial and patterned. The effect was often created by grain and pattern alone, without colour. The swirling arabesque patterns – derived from early Islamic decoration – of so-called 'seaweed' marquetry were amongst the most dramatic. Craftsmen from England, France and the Netherlands competed, but it was generally considered that the Dutch were supreme in this art. Gerrit Jensen was one of the best, and the Canons Ashby cabinet – the inside of its door pictured – is ascribed to his workshop on the grounds of the extremely high quality of the work.

Spenser's Room

Sir Erasmus Dryden's wife was a cousin of the poet Edmund Spenser. While there is only the unreliable word of the 17th-century antiquary and gossip John Aubrey that Spenser ever came to Canons Ashby, this room was named in honour of the connection.

The effect known as *enfilade* of lining up doorways in a sequence of rooms to make a grander effect, was created by Edward along his south front on both floors (see page 43 for the ground-floor *enfilade* from the Dining Room through to Sir Henry's Museum). To achieve this he had to move the doorway in Spenser's Room and introduce new doors to all the rooms. However, Spenser's Room had more than a new door.

Spenser's Room was turned from a Biblically didactic, decoratively painted withdrawing chamber into a thoroughly modern panelled bedroom, with the bed set against the Drawing Room wall, whilst fashionable carved mouldings garnished the fireplace.

Right The Elizabethan murals in Spenser's Room

Ancient and (more) modern

This might have been how it remained, had it not been for the discovery in the 1980s of the remains of Erasmus's Biblical scheme painted under the panelling on the west wall (with further scraps surviving on the east wall). A decision was taken to show the room with the ancient work exposed, but furnished as if the 18th-century scheme continued unaffected. Thus the bed, which is a reconstruction of an early 19th-century one, with the original hangings augmented by a modern imitation of scarlet moreen (cloth watered to give a shimmering effect), sits on the opposite wall.

The decorative ceiling is the sole contribution surviving today of Edward's son, Sir John, 7th (and last) Baronet of the first creation (the Drydens revived the baronetcy in 1795, see page 39). Taking the Seasons as its theme, it is rarer (and more fragile) than it appears, being composed not of plaster but of papier mâché.

Left Spenser's Room photographed by *Country Life* in 1921 before the wall paintings were uncovered

Edward's garden

Left Edward Dryden's garden to the south of the house was in the highly fashionable geometric style

Edward's transformational efforts were not limited to the house. Indeed, it is in the garden that for many the atmosphere of the place really takes hold.

J.A. Gotch, writing for *Country Life* in 1921, observed: 'Quietude is, indeed the keynote of the place, a quietude conducive to study and to the maintenance of old-fashioned, peaceful ways.' The mellow character of the ironstone walls, scattered with moss and lichens, sets the tone whilst great cedars oversee the whole.

But this was not at all what Edward had set out to do. He wanted to create a highly fashionable, highly organised and geometric layout that would reflect the latest tastes in gardening, with clean lines and manicured finishes. The object was an ordered landscape, obeying the rules of science and proportion, resulting in a garden that reflected his desires for formality in the house.

The Green Court

The garden is in two walled compartments: the Green Court forms the entrance from the Preston Capes road to the west; and the main garden to the south, descending in terraces to the Eydon road.

The Green Court was John Dryden's entrance approach, although we do not know what form it took. Edward probably introduced the topiarised yew cones and the oval sweep still discernible in the turf (although grassed over by Sir Henry in the 19th century). The gates and gate piers (pillars) are wonderful throughout the gardens, but Edward introduced some particularly fine examples here. A variety of finials top off the gate piers, including pairs of urns, a representation of the Dryden crest (a lion holding a stave) and trophies of armour, very similar in character to those painted on the fireplace board in the Great Hall.

The lead statue of a shepherd boy is cast from a model by Jan van Nost. Correspondence connects this supplier of statuary to the nobility with Edward (mention is made of a gilded gladiator as well), so it seems likely to have been made by him. Formerly positioned in the park opposite both sets of gates, it has been brought into the garden in recent years. A further example of this statue exists on the Orangery Terrace at Powis Castle.

The south garden

The doorway in the wall through to the south garden is yet another example of recycling from the monastic ruins. The south garden was Edward's main showpiece. At the bottom an avenue, recently replanted, marches away across the field. It ends on the crest of a rise, giving the impression to those viewing from the top terraces of a domain of infinite scale. Other designed views into the park, to the lakes and (from the Green Court) to the now formalised mound of the old manor were all part of Edward's landscaping. The terraces – formally identified as his 'best garden', 'upper garden', 'lower garden' and 'little one below' – started with topiary and statuary near the house, but towards the 'little one below' more mundane matters predominated, such as vegetables and fruit, but all still planted in formal patterns. A walled garden specifically for vegetables was probably a 19th-century innovation at Canons Ashby.

Above The Shepherd Boy photographed in 1906

Right Topiarised yews on the descending terraces

Victorian Revival

The member of the Dryden family who cared for Canons Ashby throughout the Victorian era had a great love of antiquity and became its careful custodian.

Pictured Canons Ashby in 1870

As Sir John had no children, despite two marriages, Canons Ashby passed to his niece, Elizabeth. Elizabeth had married John Turner of Ambrosden, in neighbouring Oxfordshire, who saw an opportunity in this unexpected inheritance. On changing his name to Dryden, he sued the Government for the revival of the defunct Dryden baronetcy and, in 1795, became Sir John Turner Dryden, 1st Baronet of the second creation. He died in 1797 of an asthma attack, having 'shone in convivial circles'.

If Elizabeth felt that her financial problems were past with the death of her spendthrift husband, her next choice was no better. Godfrey Scholey was as interested in spending his wife's money as her first husband had been, often joining with her eldest son, the new baronet, in a chorus of demands from London for more money and the settlement of bills. Sir John, the 2nd Baronet, died unmarried whilst a young man. Tragic, perhaps, to die so young, but it worked out rather well for Canons Ashby, which was inherited by his younger brother Henry, who took a more careful interest in the property.

Sir Henry the country squire

The Reverend Sir Henry was a vicar who divided his time between his parish in Ambrosden and his country estate at Canons Ashby, where he lived the life of a country squire. He evidently enjoyed his time at Canons Ashby, extolling in a letter the settled nature of life and referring to 'the even and quiet tenor of our summer existence at this sequestered spot'.

In his leisure Sir Henry enjoyed archaeology, himself undertaking excavation of the priory remains in 1828. A year later he was proposing a re-ordering of the east front of the house, commissioning drawings from a local architect called Litchfield, but the matter progressed no further than amassing piles of cut stone.

His eldest son, Sir Henry, came to be called 'the Antiquary' because of his great interest in history, and particularly in the history of his native county (although he travelled far and wide researching medieval church architecture and archaeology). Sir Henry the Antiquary came into his estate in the year that Victoria ascended the throne and died two years before she did, so his reign as squire of Canons Ashby almost precisely mirrored the reign of the queen.

Above The Reverend Sir Henry, 3rd Baronet and Vicar of Ambrosden

Sir Henry the Antiquary

Sir Henry was a polymath, nurturing interests (and considerable skill) in church music, education, architecture, archaeology and history. He was also a man of duty who fulfilled his role as the local Justice of the Peace and, in 1844, High Sheriff for the county.

Sir Henry seems to have delighted in his role as squire and keeper of his ancestral home, ensuring vagabonds travelling the lanes were always well fed in his kitchen (especially when, dressed in his customary 'scruffs', he had already met the vagrants on the road, telling them of the nourishing charity at Canons Ashby and then hurrying home to welcome his astonished guests).

He had an architect's eye for detail and a mathematician's for precision. Once, on an archaeological trip to France with friends, he insisted on returning to a site to re-measure an archaeological feature, despite an arduous detour. When asked if the extra travelling had been worthwhile, he replied, 'Oh yes, I was half an inch out.' He brought such precision to bear on drawings of all sorts of small details of his home, such as the weathervane on the tower and a window latch, measuring and drawing them with consummate skill. This unerring accuracy enabled craftsmen in 1983 to make precise copies of two pieces of Tudor furniture that he had recorded in the Kitchen at Canons Ashby, and the weathervane.

Right Sir Henry Dryden in the doorway of St Mary's

A careful custodian
Money was an ever-present concern. To save on the cost of footmen standing at table, Sir Henry had a speaking tube installed in the Dining Room so that the butler could communicate orders direct to the Kitchen. It still works. Sir Henry's father had been financially inept, but his mother was adamant that she should continue to enjoy the same standards of living in her widowhood, which had included keeping a pack of hounds. Lady Dryden did not die until 1851, which doubtless helped to postpone the marriage of her son until over a decade later.

On the house itself, he was sparing in his attentions. He blocked up some of Edward Dryden's ubiquitous sashes, replacing a pair on the east front with a small mullioned window he believed was original. He restored (as he saw it) the 'correct' Tudor approach to the house through the Pebble Court (the way visitors approach the house now). How he felt when, renewing the render decades later, he found John Dryden's original front door on the Green Court front is not recorded.

An active academic

Sir Henry seems to have been modest to the point of self-deprecation about his skills as an architect (he gave a paper to the Architectural Society in 1855, entitled 'On Mistakes Connected with Architecture, Made by Myself'). He went on to design (and build) a number of schools in local villages, cottages and stabling on the estate and a bridge. His sturdy Tudor style is well exemplified by the cottage standing beside the church with its eyebrow-like hood-moulded windows and gothic doorway. He repaired the Norwell and traced the original course of the water pipe from it to the priory and later to his own house.

Education was close to his heart. Sir Henry toured local working men's institutes and guildhalls delivering lively lectures – in which audience participation was encouraged – on architecture, archaeology and items from his own collection such as arms and armour. He was instrumental in the founding of the county library and museum in Northampton, bequeathing much of his collection to it on his death.

Family life

Sir Henry married relatively late in life – he was 47 and his bride, Frances Tredcroft (known as Fanny), the daughter of a vicar, was 42. Given their ages when they married, they might not have expected their union to be blessed with children, but in 1866 Fanny gave birth to a daughter. Alice was a bright and intelligent child, who grew up sharing her parents' interests in buildings, rural life and folklore, as well as developing her own. She took enthusiastically to photography when she was given a camera for her 21st birthday, and many of her photographs survive to give us a glimpse of their life at Canons Ashby.

Above Sketches of architectural details at Canons Ashby made by Sir Henry

Below Sir Henry and Lady Frances Dryden with their daughter Alice

A bookish man

Above The Book Room

The Book Room was so called by Sir Henry as being a room where one came to read and consult books; a library, in his estimation, was where one went to borrow them. It was the only room in the house on which Sir Henry had a marked impact.

Selected works

In the Book Room are copies of books by Dryden and Spenser as well as a signed copy of *Sir Charles Grandison* by Samuel Richardson, the father of the English novel, who was a regular visitor to Canons Ashby. Indeed, Canons Ashby makes an only slightly disguised appearance in *Sir Charles Grandison* as 'Ashby Canons'.

Today the collection is made up of a rump only of Sir Henry's books (but does include his own publications on architecture, his daughter's and the signed Richardson) with the shelves filled by the addition of a few books by and about the pioneer of the art of fly fishing, Izaak Walton, from the library at Norbury Manor and, more significantly, the parochial library on loan from Bromham parochial church council in Bedfordshire. Although little is known about the Drydens' collection of books, the founder of Bromham Library, Thomas, Lord Trevor, was of a family of similar social standing and outlook as the Drydens so, in the absence of a true Dryden library, the Bromham one is something more than a convenient stop-gap with which to fill Sir Henry's shelves.

Sir Henry kept a plan of his Book Room, in which, amongst other things, the principal contents of the cupboards are listed, including 'gardening tools' rubbing shoulders with 'medieval manuscripts'.

Doubly dubbed

It is a curiosity of Sir Henry's generation and the one after him that they bore not one, but two baronetcies (hereditary knighthoods). Not only was there the re-created Dryden baronetcy of 1795, but also, on the death of a distant cousin in 1874, Sir Henry inherited the Turner baronetcy also, thus ending up with the unusual distinction of being the 4th and 7th Baronet.

Sir Arthur Dryden, Sir Henry's nephew, passed his last days in this room in 1938, after an operation performed on a table set up in the Book Room. He had foreseen the likely need to sleep downstairs, confiding to his diary in March 1930 that: 'An electric bell was put up from the Painted Parlour to the 3rd Gallery Room, the push being in the Painted Parlour and the bell by the gallery room … that I should be able to communicate with my sister in the Brown Gallery if, as is possible, I … shall presently have to sleep in the Painted Parlour.'

Far left A sketch in oils of Sir Henry Dryden in the Book Room painted by Miss F. N. Street in 1891

No fan of formality

No formal portrait of Sir Henry exists; photographs of him in older age consistently show him dressed in wing collars, long jackets and loose-fitting trousers. He favoured a soft peaked cap, which he is to be seen wearing in many of the photographs taken by his daughter Alice. One informal portrait does exist, by Miss F. N. Street dated 1891, where the same high-collared jacket and 'nankeen' trousers are in evidence. It hangs near the door to Sir Henry's Museum.

Sir Henry's Museum

Sir Henry gathered items of natural and archaeological interest and created a small museum in what was the Painted Parlour. The original museum disappeared not long after his death in 1899, its contents dispersed amongst his various legatees, primarily the Northampton Museum, by whom the mahogany cabinet has been returned in which Sir Henry's collection used to be housed.

Left The *enfilade* effect seen on the ground floor from the Dining Room through to Sir Henry's Museum

Sir Henry's estate

In the garden the counterpoint of mown grass with spotless gravel and clipped yew had survived down to the end of the 19th century. Then came the inventions of Victorian horticulture in the shape of many flowerbeds bearing annual plantings cut into the lawn.

Indeed the garden became celebrated and was published, with plans provided by Sir Henry himself, in pioneering publications of garden history by Alicia Amherst and H. Inigo Triggs. In these, the formal elements of the garden, especially the topiary, were seen as survivals from Elizabethan times, rather than from the early 18th century. Nevertheless, Canons Ashby was influential, along with a handful of other gardens, in steering taste towards a return to formality.

By this time too, the maturity of the great cedar trees had given a gigantic scale to the garden and, with the yews, an almost mystical sense of antiquity to complement the dappled tones of the ironstone and decayed skin of the render. This appealed to the romantic nature of historians, imagining the place 'not calling for admiration ... but quietly compelling it', as J. A. Gotch opined in his article for *Country Life* in 1921.

Below The garden in Sir Henry's time

Church attendance

Sir Henry's care for the special qualities of his inheritance extended beyond the house and garden. He repaired the church, re-roofing the tower (still suffering from its firing in the Civil War) and reinstated the late medieval font (found in a ditch). This replaced Edward Dryden's sculptural stone shell font, which has been set into the garden wall on the Top Terrace.

Sir Henry's introduction of pews to replace the college-style opposed boxes that faced north and south with Sir Robert's vast table tomb between them was more radical; the boxes went to be replaced by plain oak pews of his own design and Sir Robert's tomb was demoted to a slab in the floor.

Below The 15th-century font with oak spire cover installed by Sir Henry

Above Deer in the park, photographed by Alice

Improvements in the park

In the park Sir Henry introduced a flock of Jacob's sheep to run with the deer. Their presence in Alice's photographs is a charming eccentricity that did not survive the war. Sir Henry converted a gazebo-like summer house in the park into a deer larder. Standing west of the house in the park, it has a strange, steeple-like roof and is now a private residence. The park is bounded to west and south by woodland and the lakes (formerly fish ponds). Four more lakes made up the full medieval complement, but these have silted up and are now no more than marshy areas in the woodland above the two remaining lakes. Sir Henry provided a stone animal shelter in this furthest section of the park; its twin stands in the paddock.

The end of an era

Sir Henry's long stewardship of Canons Ashby combined the care and concern for detail of a curator with the characterful life of a Victorian squire, ruling his little fiefdom with a zeal for the place and its people perhaps unusual in his class. His death in 1899 marked the end of an era, followed by a period of long, slow decline that only ended with a last-minute rescue nearly 100 years later.

A time of gentle decline

Alice Dryden's photographs from the 1880s and 1890s illustrate her proficiency with a camera and also provide a wonderfully evocative record of Canons Ashby at this time.

Alice inherited her father's love of history, publishing books on needlework and new editions of medieval treatises on hunting (no doubt inheriting some of that interest from her grandmother). She moved to London on her father's death and, marrying late in life, settled in Highclere near Newbury with her husband, John Marcon.

Before the Great War

Sir Henry was succeeded by his brother Alfred, a barrister who lived in Putney. He continued to practise the law for a few years before coming to live permanently at Canons Ashby, his childhood home.

He undertook some stonework and render repairs on the house in 1906, employing the architect J. A. Gotch, who was later to rhapsodise on the charms of Canons Ashby in the pages of *Country Life*. He embellished the two splendid oak garden seats that Edward had had made for the garden terraces with painted canopies to ward off unwanted breezes.

A widower, his house was kept for him by his unmarried daughters Mary and Clara. The latter was the second family chronicler of the house and its estate in as many generations, but in watercolour rather than photographs. Her charming sketches decorate the house to this day, offering every conceivable view of Canons Ashby, often blanketed in snow and ice, which commonly afflicts this land-locked county in winter.

Sir Arthur's enduring legacy to the place is his creation of wrought-iron gates for the garden and park entrances. Prior to these, apart from the 18th-century pair in the Green Court, the gates seem to have been a mixture of more or less informal wooden farm gates.

Below St Mary's Church photographed by Alice in 1880

Changing society

When Sir Alfred died in 1912 he was succeeded by his eldest son, Arthur. Sir Arthur, the 6th and 9th Baronet, kept an estate diary recording life on a gently declining estate. It offers interesting insights into the changes to society resulting from the Great War, such as: 'August 22 1916. Finished hay harvest. A very bountiful crop.... The groom, under gardener & shepherd the only men at work, one woman employed, the rest done by self, sisters and maids.'

He also left clues that would prove valuable to later custodians of Canons Ashby: 'April 1929. During this month the two servants' bedrooms ... were re-whitened.... In one part of the larger one, under the old paper, was found the remains of a kind of fresco representing a larger room. This was retained uncovered as far as possible and left otherwise untouched.'

A royal visit

In her declining years Queen Mary, the widow of George V, used to pass the time staying with friends in the country and, for amusement, invite herself to old and curious country houses in the area. The queen was rumoured to have kleptomaniac tendencies, helping herself to antique trinkets, making her an even more formidable guest for many country house owners. She graced Canons Ashby with her presence in 1937 – there is a photograph of the elderly Clara Dryden bidding the royal guest farewell – but whether she took with her a souvenir of her visit is not recorded.

Above *Alfred Dryden Taking Tea in the Hall 1911*, by Clara Dryden

Left A watercolour of the Pebble Court painted by Clara Dryden

Far left Sir Alfred with his daughters Clara and Mary

Difficult decisions

The housekeeping arrangements continued with Clara and Mary in charge until the cataclysmic winter of 1937/38, when not only did Sir Arthur die, but also his younger brother and both of his unmarried sisters.

Only one sister, Louisa, married to Major Pritchard, survived. Of her three sons, the youngest, Cecil, was the sole survivor of the First World War. So it was left to Cecil, who changed his name to Dryden in 1939, to shoulder the responsibility for Canons Ashby on his mother's death in 1948. However, Cecil had made his life in Rhodesia (now Zimbabwe) and on his death in 1959, his three sons, Peter, John and Douglas, decided to stay in Africa.

Below A wintry scene at Canons Ashby, painted by Clara Dryden

Above Cecil Pritchard, who changed his name to Dryden on inheriting Canons Ashby

An artist in residence

Canons Ashby, much reduced by death duties and the house largely emptied by the family's removal to Africa, was let to a series of tenants. One of the most colourful of these was the architect and goldsmith Louis Osman, who used the house as his workshop and his home from the late 1960s to 1979. It was here that he designed and created, using the new process of electroforming, the gold crown that was used for the investiture of HRH The Prince of Wales in 1969. Other commissions included a gold and enamel casket housing a copy of the Magna Carta to celebrate the Bicentennial of the Independence of the United States in 1976.

Osman came to specialise in works of art in gold and surprised his neighbours in rural Northamptonshire with a one-man show held in the Long Gallery, which comprised 131 separate pieces created by him and his craftsmen.

A surprising turn of events

The structural problems of the house had begun to gallop and Osman, a great artist, designer and architect but never a businessman, made little attempt to tackle them. The house was always freezing cold and an invitation to lunch there involved several layers of overcoats to keep warm in the draughts of the Great Hall. Diners used to take it in turns to sit near the fire.

Osman used the Servants' Hall as his workshop, flicking off slivers of the later paint layers to reveal tiny parts of the heraldic scheme below for his astonished visitors, whilst his wife, Dilys Roberts, a fine enameller, worked in the little ante-chamber next door.

Osman left when bankruptcy beckoned, removing to another, smaller and more remote country house on the Welsh borders, where he continued to create beautiful things and run chaotic finances. Meanwhile, matters were coming to a head for the old house. The three Dryden brothers needed a new tenant for the house and had accepted an offer from a company that wanted to operate Canons Ashby as a hotel and residential conference centre, once devoid of its contents. It was then that the National Trust got involved.

Below Louis Osman, long-term tenant of Canons Ashby, pictured with one of his most famous commissions, the crown used for the investiture of HRH The Prince of Wales

The Rescue of
Canons Ashby

Canons Ashby came close to destruction in the 1980s. The story of its rescue is one of dedication, sacrifice and generosity.

Gervase Jackson-Stops, architectural historian and Architectural Adviser to the National Trust from 1975, grew up in the countryside around Canons Ashby. It was a property he paid particular attention to, becoming more and more concerned by its slow decline. When he heard in June 1980 of the impending sale of the remaining contents of Canons Ashby before its lease as a hotel, he was determined to try to save it and its contents.

Working with his senior colleague, Martin Drury, who later became Director General of the National Trust, he cooked up a plan to rescue and restore the house, gardens and church, and also provide the much-needed endowment for the long-term care of the property. The plan was ambitious. It relied not only on the agreement of the Dryden family to part with Canons Ashby, but also on the Monument Fund, the interest of the Landmark Trust and the backing of the newly formed National Heritage Memorial Fund. This would be the first time the National Trust was proactive in directly approaching owners; but everyone realised that this would be the last chance for the house.

A group effort

Initially, John Dryden, the Dryden brother appointed to negotiate by his family, was reticent about the family giving up the property. But the promise of limited opening to visitors and a flat for the use of members of the family whenever they were in England swayed him.

Even so, with negotiations barely begun, the sale of contents had to go ahead as planned. However, thanks to the generous support of the Monument Fund, nearly everything was acquired that had been selected. In the meantime, the Landmark Trust had pledged £100,000 towards the costs of restoring the house in return for a flat in the upper reaches of the tower to be run as a holiday let. Most significantly, the National Heritage Memorial Fund agreed to give £1,500,000 towards endowment and repairs. In addition, the Historic Buildings Council agreed a 70 per cent grant towards the repair of the house and church.

With all of this confirmed and a public appeal launched (which would go on to raise £350,000) the Dryden family agreed to give the house, church, paddock and gardens to the National Trust along with a lease over 65 acres of parkland. All of this was achieved in a remarkably short space of time so that, in December 1980, six months after the crisis first arose, John Dryden was able to write a charming letter of thanks to the Director General of the National Trust. None of which would have happened without the energy and enthusiasm of the late Gervase Jackson-Stops.

Opposite The restored house and garden

Below Gervase Jackson-Stops photographed with the Leconfield Aphrodite at Petworth

Major repairs

The house appeared to be in an advanced state of decay. Signs of rot, both wet and dry, were evident all over the place and the roof was leaking in many different areas.

What's more, the south front was bowing out alarmingly, threatening to bring down the whole façade and with it the unique vaulted plaster ceiling of the Drawing Room.

The condition of the church was, in many ways, even worse with fissures opening between nave and aisle and the pinnacles on top of the tower ready to collapse. The garden was like a jungle and the coach house had lost its roof to a fire.

However, the report by the architect, Rodney Melville, was surprisingly optimistic, acknowledging that, although there was much to repair, the basic structure of the house was good and would respond.

Conservation and discovery

A three-year programme of work followed with major interventions in the roof of the south range to hold the plaster ceiling, whilst Edward Dryden's outer skin of ashlar stonework was painstakingly knitted back to the 16th-century core. The render on the tower proved to be losing adhesion and had to be replaced (in the process evidence was found, in the form of a cigarette packet, of repairs being undertaken in the 1930s). In the north wing decades of leaking roofs and lack of ventilation had provided the perfect conditions for dry rot, which had become rampant and had to be eradicated.

Above Canons Ashby clad in scaffolding and straggly yews in the Green Court

The painted panelling in the Servants' Hall was carefully stripped of its over-layers and conserved, and the extraordinary discoveries of the 16th-century painted scheme in Spenser's Room and the 18th-century painted reredos in the church were made.

Complex conservation challenges were faced in dealing with the contents, none more so than the Green Cloth in the Great Hall with its fragile silk embroidered coat of arms and silvered frame, filthy from smoke and damaged by sunlight.

Completing the set

In July 1980 the Trust's Historic Building Secretary, Martin Drury, received a phone call concerning a set of embroidered chairs that had been bought by Edward Dryden in the early 18th century. The set had left Canons Ashby in 1936 but had just reappeared on the market and had been sold at auction in Bath for £15,000. For a week Martin pursued the set as it ran through the chain of furniture dealers, working its way to the top of the trade, where he finally tracked it down at Mallett's in Bond Street. In a matter of five days the price had risen more than six-fold. Accepting that this is what happens when extremely important items enter the market for the first time in living memory, Martin negotiated the price down a little, but in effect that was what the Monument Fund and the Victoria & Albert Museum between them had to find to ensure the set returned to Canons Ashby. The chairs are now on display in the Tapestry Room (pictured on pages 30 and 31).

Ready to be revealed

All of this and much more was achieved in a little over three years. Items of the collection were returned from Africa and loaned by members of the family to the property and, additionally, family portraits returned from their temporary home in the Northamptonshire Records Office. Canons Ashby was now ready to be opened to the public, which it did for the first time in April 1984. Michael Heseltine, then Secretary of State for the Environment, visited to declare it the first great success of the National Heritage Memorial Fund.

Above Repairing the dangerously sagging Drawing Room ceiling in 1981

Left White paint being removed in the Servants' Hall in the 1980s to reveal decoration below

Back to Baroque

By the time the National Trust had completed the renovation works to the house, the gardens had suffered many years of neglect. The topiary was overgrown and the once gravel paths had so much grass they were maintained by mowing.

Enough of the Baroque layout survived to make a full-scale restoration worthwhile, though, for financial reasons, this had to wait until 2007. Before the restoration work began, a huge amount of archive research was carried out. In the family papers a 19th-century drawing of the garden was found with measurements by Sir Henry. There were also photographs by his daughter, Alice, and another set found dating from 1921.

Archaeological work was also commissioned, including a geophysical survey, which revealed some details of the 16th-century garden. After the research was complete, in collaboration with Historic England, it was decided to restore both the Baroque bones of the garden, including the topiary, and the 19th-century plantings that had softened its formality.

The revived design

The garden front of the house faces south-west. Below it descend four layers of terrace, each level demarcated by topiary yews. The Top Terrace and the Sundial Terrace below both have lawns inset with geometric flowerbeds. These had been covered over but were reinstated and are planted with spring or summer bedding. There are further beds against the walls, accessed by gravel paths and planted as late 19th-century herbaceous borders.

On the lower two terraces, gravel changes to grass for the paths, which lead down into two levels of vegetable and fruit gardens. Cardoons, sunflowers and runner beans on tripods give height to beds edged with lavender in this relaxed interpretation of a Victorian cutting and vegetable garden.

To the side of the top two terraces are lawned areas. On the lower one the Victorian rose garden (known as the Mulberry Lawn) has been recreated, though with four beds instead of the original two; while the top one is dominated by a huge Cedar of Lebanon, planted in 1780.

Below left The garden overgrown

Below right A stone pier in the corner of the Green Court under restoration

Opposite The Sundial Terrace today

The Baroque gates

Other than the overall formality of his garden, Edward Dryden made clear his taste for the Baroque in strikingly ornate gates set between piers, or pillars, topped with finely fashioned finials. Helping to bring the garden back to its early 18th-century design, a fortuitous discovery was made in the burnt-out shell of the stables in 1981: a pair of badly damaged but still recognisable wooden Baroque gates. These are incredibly rare survivals. Although repaired and hung in 1984, they have deteriorated so much that it has been decided to reproduce them, keeping the originals safe out of the weather. The gate piers with their scrolled finials were copied for the entrance court at Chequers by Lord Lee, as he repaired that house in 1920 prior to handing it over for use by Prime Ministers.

Caring for Canons Ashby and its future

In October 1828, in a letter to a friend, the Reverend Sir Henry Dryden laid out his philosophy and pride in his family and Canons Ashby.

'But under any difficulties … you will submit to much before you part with a single acre. One of my greatest objects in life is to clear and disencumber my family property to make it better and somewhat more extensive than I found it, & to leave to my descendants an estate which, without allowing scope for ambition or luxury, shall enable them to maintain with respectability & independence, their station as English gentry.'

Generosity of spirit

In many ways this expresses the feelings at the heart of the family and the soul of this place. We are fortunate indeed that the three Dryden brothers chose the National Trust to care for, explain and reveal the beauties and the complexities of their home. The National Trust's understanding of the house, estate and its people continues to grow, always with the encouragement of the Dryden family. Douglas, the last of the brothers, died in 2014, but the succeeding generations continue to support the National Trust in its care of their family home.

The Drydens' act of generosity will ensure that the stories and histories at Canons Ashby will continue to be revealed and shared with those who want to come and discover the quiet delights of Canons Ashby.

Above Canons Ashby remains and will always remain a place of rural tranquillity